SPEAKING WORDS

Writing for Reading Aloud

GW00726044

An anthology e...... ..,
Deborah Tyler-Bennett

Crystal Clear Creators (CCC) Publishing

SPEAKING WORDS

Contents

Preface – Deborah Tyler-Bennett, editor, p.9

Words for Whispering

Words for Speaking

Words for Shouting

Words for Singing

Words for Performing

Preface

Speaking Words, Speaking Voices

Sing whatever is well made.
W.B. Yeats, 'Under Ben Bulben' (1938)

In 2005 Crystal Clear Creators hosted a series of day writing workshops at Loughborough University's Department of English and Drama, BBC Radio Leicester, and Monks' Dyke Technology College, Lincolnshire. These events were facilitated by a varied programme of tutors including Jonathan Taylor, Mitzi Szereto, Julie Boden, Maria Orthodoxou, Peter Lewis, and myself. The great thing about day workshops (as any creative writer involved in them will tell you) is that you never know what sort of writing they will engender. The outcome of the creative workshop cannot be planned for, and is, thus, fascinating. Sometimes, the most frustrating element of work-shopping is that the writing produced is of a potentially high quality but, unless the writer decides to work on it and then send it to a little magazine, goes largely unseen. The outcomes of a day school can vanish into the ether, and fade from memory. Therefore, when I was asked to edit a collection of work polished and crafted after the Crystal Clear events, I was delighted. I was even more pleased when I read the collection of work submitted, and realised the sheer variety of writing. Choosing the following selection of pieces was an interesting task in itself, and it was impossible to include all submissions for the anthology in the final text.

The idea of an anthology meant for reading aloud establishes a key function of the writer's craft. Most writers read work aloud at almost every stage of its creation. The sections of this anthology suggest tones of reading. Some words are better spoken softly, whilst others are meant to be shouted aloud, some imply a chant that is close to song, and still more should be spoken. In 1928 the Traveller's Library issued a volume edited by Edward Thomas prior to his death in 1917, entitled *Poems and Songs for the Open Air* which encouraged the reading aloud of poems in the open, so perhaps this volume is part of a tradition which implies the oral function of writing. The sections in the volume represent my choices of tone – the reader may have other ideas as to how the works included can be read.

Diversity is, I think, one of the pleasures of an anthology such as this. Leigh Chia's gothic city fitted well with Sue Mackrell's vision of Prague, and this, in turn, contrasted with the time-ridden landscapes implied by David Bircumshaw. Robin Hamilton's dialect poems give us a vital burst of Glaswegian, especially when this meets the ancient tale of *Beowulf*, whilst Jonathan Taylor re-figures the children's story with a semi-epistolary tale, and both Mark Goodwin and Nathan Vaughan go for more shadowy and sinister images in poetry and prose.

Speaking words imply speaking voices, and I was struck by the robust dialects and contrasting rhythms of many of the works included here (texts that go from poetry to monologue, and from short story to adaptation). Comedy, chanting, elegiac tones, unorthodox love songs, and mixed concerts, all find their way into this anthology. As do stories of different cultural worlds – from Africa to Scotland, and from Arab landscapes to supernatural cars. The idea of an anthology as a magic box, 'rattle-bag' (to borrow a phrase from Ted Hughes and Seamus Heaney), or literary market-place of colourful stalls all vying for attention, became more appealing the more I studied the work submitted. So here is the result, an eclectic selection of poetry, stories, monologues, and adaptations, which gave me pleasure to re-visit, and reminded me of the unknown, and truly creative, quality of the writing workshop.

Deborah Tyler-Bennett, 2005

1: WORDS FOR WHISPERING

She filled my quiet house with words.

George Mackay Brown, 'The Five Voyages of Arnor'

Sepulchral City

The dead-end road, hosting
Fresh tarmac, strangely invigorating.
Brittle shoes, stepping
On operatic pathways, parading.

Horrid faces, a hullabaloo,
Their eyes gawping
At me, penetrating through.
Running up trees, towering.

Looking in, I am consumed,
Peculiar smells arouse my curiosity
Like addictive perfume, leading
To a secret sepulchral city.

Leigh Chia

Prague Night

As the Prague night lengthens and stretches, the true nature of the city reasserts itself. The Old Town retreats into its past, the narrow alleys and dark passages, the web of streets, intersections leading to dead ends, walls leaning inwards, claustrophobic and menacing, dark shadows, underground passages and dank, stone vaulted cellars. Stories of mystery and horror and intrigue have frightened strangers away for centuries, while deals are done, and payment is taken … the wicked Turk who cut off the head of his lover, leaving her spectre to haunt the streets, stories of fear and revenge, a warning to women, "keep to your own," stories to frighten outsiders, to feed dread and terror in streets haunted by cut-throats and thieves, the withered arm in the church, they say it was cut off by the Virgin Mary in a heavenly act of revenge for stealing church treasure, the streets lined with butchers' shops, where one more piece of flesh goes unnoticed.

In the Old Square the puppets dance grotesquely, stiff-limbed, their joints locked in convulsive contortions, Don Quixote and Turks and gypsies, and gold-robed kings. Pierrot and a black malevolent devil join hands to ape the macabre jerkings of their automaton compatriots in the Old Clock, urged on by the puppet master St Vitus. The apostles and the Saviour march through the open doors; death, the skeleton tempts the miser; the miser spurns death – and at cock-crow they all vanish. The clockmaker had his eyes gouged out so that there would never be another. The clock chimes give way to the faint strains of the hurdy-gurdy, stock in trade of the itinerant puppeteers, with their travelling theatres. If the Nazis didn't get them the communists did …. Outside Mozart's theatre, Don Giovanni broods, faceless under his hood. In Kafka's house, cockroaches scuttle in the dark, black shiny carapaces, claws scratching the stone floors.

The Jewish cemetery groans with its weight of gravestones leaning inwards, falling, ancient diseased teeth, decomposing.   Elder trees roots scrabble amongst the desiccated skeletons, a palimpsest of generations lost, twelve cadavers deep. Sarcophagi are inscribed with Talmudic hieroglyphs, graves of Rabbis, Cohens, with carvings of blessing hands, tailors, their graves inscribed with scissors. Rabbi Loew lies here, hubristic creator of the Golem, his tabernacle inscribed with labyrinths. Small stones are piled on the graves, no flowers, just bare stones in remembrance of the desert, stones to stop wolves and lions from scrabbling up the bones, eating the body, stones to mark the grave of a loved one.

The Hebrew clock turns anti-clockwise, against the sun, winding back the hours to the middle ages, to the Old New Synagogue, where the massacre left indelible stains of blood on the walls, and the passage is called Red Lane recalling the cobbles and gutters thick with it. On the air still hangs a haunting Yiddish tune, a dying Hebrew prayer. In his lair in the roof space the Golem crouches, a clay homunculus created by cabalistic ritual, circling and chanting, talismanic, magical; the *shem*, a shred of parchment bearing the unpronounceable, all-powerful name of God is placed in his mouth. He takes his first breath. But the *shem* must be removed on the Sabbath. One Friday night Rabbi Loew forgets. Once a creature of servitude, the Golem becomes rebellious, enraged, goes beserk. He may still lurk in that roof space ... the mad creature in the attic, the metaphor for the mad in all of us.

Sue Mackrell

Entropy, Horology, Maps

In my mother's house as the end approached
        the clocks were always wrong, as
if time had dishevelled itself of the illusion of
        order, unsynchronising
longitude and latitude into a scatterful of
        unpacked cards. A lottery had
fallen through the roof of her mind and it gave
        no winning numbers. Tock.

Tick. I would look at the silver birches and the
        dog-roses in the grounds
and through the alphabets of branches read the
        accents of the skies: the
slivers of moon that fattened through the
        month, the diamond drill-points of
stars, the figures that assembled against the
        handwriting of leaves. Es ist ein. Ding.

Dong. Too long had assembled in her space. At
        night she talked to the past,
complaining, arguing, asserting as I'd lay
        listening, helpless as a tear, in

my room. So far fallen. Stardust we all en. 's
     lost solez uz weighfearen way
frum 'um. Tick.

Tock. The rocking horse rocked.

David Bircumshaw

KLIM

he told me he was leaving ...
Haleeb is a constant daily diet
he told me he will be back ...
Haleeb is bought from *Ha'aj* Mohammed
he told me to take care ...
Haleeb is the preferred nutrient for the bones
he told me he will always love me...
...spewed out the KLIM...
...once again I drink my milk...

Maha Mahmoud

Haleeb *is the Arabic word for milk*
Ha'aj *is the Arabic title given to person who
performed the pilgrimage* Hajj *to Mecca.*

Do you want to be here?

Do you want to be here?

Close your eyes,
Picture what I tell you
And I will magically transport you there.

Thick legged, minute spiders judder
Across the paved path, dissecting
This wild, wild place.

I notice them only because,
Every now and again,
I check the route I'm taking
Instinctively drawn forward
To nowhere in particular,
Just the next place.

Dead, split trees stand guard
Along the way, staring down with
Their stern appearance,
Watching us, carefully,
For wraiths and strays,
To pick off and consume in their hollow trunks,
Taking them Worlds away from this place.

I could try to describe the colours and shapes
That surround me, but would my words be enough?

Squirrels playing in a tree
Making me giggle as they precariously balance

To reach the nuts at the end of the thinning branch,
Till the tip dips too low.

Shy deer becoming tame.
Their beautiful eyes less startled,
More curious.
What have I in my bag that they could eat?
Disney cartoons embedding images of
Grace and cuteness in our minds,
The reality more moving and vivid.

So come to this place,
Our place.

Louise Pymer

Sea Requiem – Valentia Island, South West Ireland

In memory of David John

Whale backed surge of the Atlantic,
Oceanic arc of molten glass
Breaks and shatters against the
Granite crags, elemental, awe-ful power
Climaxing
And withdrawing
Sliding back over shingle,
Elision of sea and land,
A shifting of boundaries.

The ancients anthropomorphised the unknown,
The fearful, the unfathomable,
Poseidon, Manannan, Neptune,
But if the ocean is a god it is surely hermaphrodite,
A fusion of that masculine power
And the fertile, hypnotic rhythm,
An amniotic fluid which nurtures creation,
Throbbing protonic particles splitting and mutating,
Creating the moment of the first amphibian
Bridging the boundaries of water and land,
Generating outlandish creatures which terrified
          and enthralled,
Reality fusing with fantasy,
The erotic longings of ancient sailors
Transposed into sirens and mermaids
Luring men to their death in an orgasmic sea,
Drawn down in the unconscious realms,
Watched by the wise, sorrowful eyes of seals,
The souls of the drowned.

Humans attribute their own emotions,
Anger, hatred, vengeance, fear,
To the magnitude of the sea,
But its power lies in its supreme indifference,
Implacable to the insignificance of humans
          swept into its depths,
Sometimes giving up these sacrifices,
Sometimes withholding them.

Their memorial is in the
Radiance of the sunlight
Glittering on the bright white foam,
The shifting deep sapphire blue,

The steel grey and the turquoise,
And the momentary rainbows
Glimpsed in the silver wind blown cascades of
    spindrift.

Sue Mackrell

Monsieur le Directeur

I demand I desist from your service today.
What is its name *je ne connais pas* but let it
become *Alphinor*. There is a lighthouse
that says that in my head. Rocks

to your monthly bills, your fuckface threats
of final notice, dusk. I have accompted my
    inventories
with the snub patience of chalk. Item:
2 tusks *d'ivoire* (& guns for Makonnen) Item: 5
    fingers

of nibs, snotted with dried ink. Item:
a lace sheet on a Belgian postcard, lightly
penned with blood. Item: a fusillade of vowels.
Item: seven volumes, unbound, of left luggage,
    verbs.

I leave for Suez tomorrow. By *Alphinor*, in a black
    hull.
Item: a street dog's cough. There is something
    bad

sailing in my blood, no illumination lights
in nursing eyes. Tell me the time (*Item*) I must
    be

shouldered on board.

9 November, 1891. Marseille.

David Bircumshaw

Congenital Sunshine

A really courageous sunflower,
(if it wishes to be recognised as its parents'
offspring)
will be of a colour so painfully yellow
that a pair of eyes, on seeing it,
will draw down their lids in self protection:
But the unrelenting, piercing pigment of that
sunflower,
(if it wishes to maintain family tradition)
will burn its dazzling image
into their secret, shaded place.

Susan Bell

Love is not to be found

Love is not to be found
in worldly talk or gestures;
I have found love and it is
shaped, gently, like your smile,
it speaks with your voice,
and in your hands I have felt
the tenderness of its touch
upon my skin.

Love has painted me in shades
of radiance. It has made me more
than the person I am.
Alone I am low and bereft, yet
with you and the love which binds me
I am more than stars and earth.

Maria D. Orthodoxou

You know you've got a cold

You know when you've got a cold
                                Uh huh
and you're all blocked up and stuffy
                                hmmm
and you can't breathe
                                yes ...
that's how I am.

                              Colds are just
                              temporary, an ailment
                              that passes quickly
Not this one
                              I'll make you some
                              hot, creamy soup to
                              soothe you
it won't help, I'm congested
                              I can get some Lemsip
                              – it will clear your
                              head
but when we get into bed my chest feels heavy
                              what about some
                              vapour rub? – I'll
                              massage it in nice and
                              gentle
it makes my eyes water
                              I have some tissues
                              for you, balmy and soft
my nose is too sore already.

Your voice is ringing over and over in my ears
                              I'll whisper softly

but you can't hear me, you won't listen

> *I am my love, you*
> *must be tired*

I've got a rose stem in my throat, the thorns are
scratchy and painful

> *I'll be the medicine, I*
> *can coat your neck,*
> *cling and nourish it*

there is no remedy.

> *Then come into bed*
> *and we'll watch the fire*

I can't sleep, I have a temperature.

> *Cosy and warm.*

Stifling and uncomfortable.

> *Give me a kiss – it*
> *won't be contagious ....*
>
> *Victoria Rose Poolman*

On the Street

A saxophone drowns the street
In a remembered tune
Crowds of faces
Lined with different songs
Rivers searching
Ears contorted with different voices
Waves spreading, speaking
Eyes a universe of suns
Falling away in reflections
One face
One sun dropping over the horizon
Crowded with the stillness of recollection
A face of tears
Sun shocked
Memory falling under finger taps
She dreams the song
Rain falling all over the street
Echoing worlds, worlds, worlds.

Mark Pullinger

2: WORDS FOR SPEAKING

I hear leaves drinking rain ...

                    - W. H. Davies, 'Rain'

To Read

As I sit here
Staring at the page as I sit here
I know nothing
The books that barricade my departure from the desk
Tease and taunt
They know
They exist
They have consumed their knowledge
And bequeathed it to their pages
They speak
In Greek
Bleak and nondescript
They nonetheless hold a power
That raises them to gods
I have no voice
I cannot utter a mutter
Muster a whisper
I sigh
Cry
And through my tears
Comes the meaning I desire
I desire
I pick a book from off the shelf
And pull its pages to me
Hungry for their print
The off-white paper chafes my fingertips
As I caress the sultry ink
To read
To live
To love

I lay my face upon the page
And smell the cool scent of desire
The words yearn to be read
The tale longs to be said
Read me
Be me
Lose yourself in me and question your desires
I tear a curl of paper from the page
And put it to my lips
It rolls upon my tongue
And stains my teeth with musk
The heady perfume draws me to a new world
A world of exploration
A journey
A quest
I am lost in the shadows
And in my loss I call to the mother who has left me
But it is not she who answers
The voice that returns like an echo is not hers
Instead I taste the blood of the writer
As she offers me her heart
With the same knife I cut myself
And bleed into the book.

Xanthe Wells

1717

Robert 'Roy' MacGregor

Donald Glas blooded me at Killicrankie.
This father I honoured at Callander.
From Forth to Stirling they hunted me
then I was captured, taken at Balquhidder.

I've sheltered in Breadelbane's Finlarig Castle,
and been a battling Jacobite at Sheriffmuir,
but young Mary Campbell of Comer called –
then I was captured, returned to Balquhidder.

Mary MacGregor

My ferocious forefathers of Balloch
executed Gregor Roy, chief of clan;
our sworn enemies, Colquohoun conquerors,
mixed MacGregor and Cambell at Breadelbane.

The Colquohouns and William of Orange
unnamed the Auchinsallen warrior.
My love languished in Logierait,
before surrendering, for his honour.

The Marquis of Montrose

That common reiver Rob 'Roy' MacGregor
expects blind faith in highwayman days.

I've known him as prosperous proprietor,
invested grandly in his big outlays.
He gives his word as if a legal bond,
A contract sealed by the cut of his sword.
Duncan MacDonald strayed beyond
Clan honour, to take my loan as his horde.
I, Montrose, must have my money;
Craigrostan and MacGregor's blood,
broached by Boquhan, outlawed, runny,
left his wife, bubbling my name in its flood.
His clan starves on, each wife, child and beggar,
under the watchful ghost of Donald MacGregor.

Iain MacGregor (ghost, died 1701)

We went from cattle to battle at Killicrankie,
warrior Donald Glas and clan MacGregor.
John Graham's Jacobites against mighty Mackay.
1689, and no thoughts of Balquhidder.

The Lennox Watch was not yet our livelihood,
enemy Campbells now our marriage blood
    brothers,
our twenty-five hundred beat Mackay's four
    thousand.
1689, and no thoughts of Balquhidder.

Donald Glas MacGregor (ghost, died 1702)

I blooded my boys at Killicrankie,
before I was prisoner in Edinburgh,

I, Donald Glas, garrulous Jacobite,
died before Rob Ruadh's capture at Balquhidder.

I blooded my boys at Killicrankie,
to teach them to honour the Clan MacGregor.
My boy Rob Roy married his Campbell-bred
cousin,
and she recaptured him at Balquhidder.

Radcliff Gregory

Snow Queen and City Guardian

Once, not too long ago, but definitely far away,
there was a city. The city was full of
department stores, bars, churches, and T.V.
repair shops. City people lived, as city people
do, from day to day, clutching mobiles, running
for buses, trams, and trains, and wearing down
their shoe heels.

It was November, in the shops Christmas
decorations had been up for three months, and
the Snow Queen, travelling north to visit her
sister, stopped at the highest point of the city.
She stopped partly for a rest and partly (as
witches on-the-go seldom rest) to blow white
flakes over roof-gardens, church towers, and
sky-scrapers. "They're like white wasps," said a
woman hurrying to buy Lotto tickets. As the
Snow Queen blew, the city was soon blanketed

in royal icing.   She began to contemplate whether it would be worth turning a few people's hearts to ice before she left, just for fun.

Now, the highest point of the city was a cemetery, long unused, full of old monuments and memorials. Urns and angels, clasped hands and weeping women, were ranged against the wintering sky. The mausoleums got to be more like mansions the closer to the top of the hill they came. Having lived for centuries, the Snow Queen was a very observant witch, and said aloud: "Did no poor people ever live here? The tombs get grander the more one looks."

"Alas," responded a hollowed voice: "the poor were buried outside the city walls. Even now, when there is a smart new cemetery within city limits, the paupers' graves are in a far-off field, sometimes marked by tiny wooden crosses, sometimes, I weep to say, unmarked." The Snow Queen gazed round icily. She always got irritated by interruptions. They were not regal.

No one.

Only the massive, obsidian, statue of an angel, one hand reaching for the sky, the index finger broken. Snow caped his shoulders and his blank eyes gazed to where flakes danced. A plinth below the angel bore the words 'The City Guardian.' As he spoke again, his voice seemed to come from deep within the earth. "Yesterday," it said, "a man was buried in a cardboard coffin, like a big filing-box. The only mourners were two county-council workers who had failed to trace his family, and they claimed their attendance on expenses."

"Did they bring flowers?" asked the Queen, who was getting bored by the angel's moral tone. There was a huge creak as the angel's head moved from side to side in denial. "A pity, I like flowers, at least, white ones. And tell me this, angel, did not one person in the city ever weep for the man while he was alive? Wonder what had become of him? Search?" Again, a mighty creaking.

"No one, but a vicar wanting his lunch, and rushing through the ceremony, said one word above the grave," sighed the angel, "and, if anyone had once cared, I never discovered them."

"Such hard hearts," said the Snow Queen, whose interest had suddenly been restored. "I must thank you," she continued, smiling through teeth that glittered like a jeweller's window.

"Thank me?" The angel's voice rang with concern.

"Yes. I was here for a rest before moving on, but I was contemplating turning a few hearts to ice before I left, a girl must do something to justify herself, you know. But … " again the smile would have out-shone platinum, "I see you've icy hearts a plenty here, with a little work, I can freeze the whole city. If a man can die totally un-mourned, and with no one to say a kind word for him, how easy it will be to harden the remaining soft hearts of the city. So you see, I think your story has persuaded me to stay. This is my city, now."

"Your hand on the breast will harden hearts, but it will take years to freeze the whole city," the angel mused.

"Oh, how sweetly old fashioned of you, to think I still work personally. As if I'd want to touch them!" said the Snow Queen with a rattling laugh. "No, I make hundreds of ice blue mobile phones manifest themselves in all the shops, but, before that, adverts appear for them everywhere, as if by magic, of course. On tubes ... buildings ... buses ... on the web. People go crazy for them. By the time they appear, the whole city's mine. One finger on them and that's it. They're also picture phones, the more you stare into them the harder you become. I update every two months, and there you are. Once you have one, you'll always want the latest. Clever, eh? Speaking of which, I must start, or I'll never make a city fit for me to live in, my sister can visit me this time, it's her turn, actually." She was gone in a whirl of feathers.

Above the city, the angel listened. He listened for two days. Nothing. Maybe she had changed her mind. Then, the buzz began. It began with a film projected onto the side of a building – a beautiful woman with blonde hair and a kingfisher-hued cape, bearing more than a passing resemblance to the Snow Queen herself. Her turquoise painted nails tapped at an ice blue plastic rectangle, and she breathed the words: "I want one!" from the wall in vapour. Then buses, tubes, and broadband all began to glisten with her image. In the shops, blue cloths began to appear, with a countdown of three days taking place behind them. Outside, the frenzy grew. PEOPLE CRUSHED IN QUEUE FOR NEW ICE BLUE MOBILE, the papers rang. PHONES SOLD OUT BEFORE THEY HIT SHOPS. Within a few days of their arrival, almost everyone in the city had an ice blue phone, and those that did not want them had been bought one by relatives. People robbed to get phones, and city beggars always seemed to find one that someone had dropped. And then, her work was done, and the Snow Queen moved in to the most expensive hotel in the city, indefinitely.

Up on his mount, the angel heard the click of empty conversations, sounding like the chink of a million crystal glasses. He heard women and men on dates ignore their lovers to speak to whoever was at their phone's end. He heard children talk to each other about the latest war games and how many characters they killed each day. He realised that down there, people had stopped looking into each others' eyes, and became aware that what he heard less and less was the light sound of human laughter. The angel's dark lids closed over his bald eyes. He could protect the city no longer.

There was a mighty crack. The angel's gleaming black body cleaved in two as if it was a lightning-struck oak. His pointing hand still outstretched, indicated a great rush of air that rose into the morning sky. A thousand blue-black crows shot from the sundered body, to roar, wheeling, cawing, and flopping, over their wing-darkened city. Then the crows were gone, and the angel crumbled to dust in an instant.

Surveying her city from the air, the Snow Queen noticed the crater that had opened up where the city's guardian angel had once stood. Swooping into it, she giggled at his demise. Then she noticed, on the ground, a small metal heart, about the size of a bead. "He didn't have such a big heart after all," she pouted, lifting the object and popping it in her mouth. At once, a strange warmth suffused her, and her eyes grew wet. "Pah!" she retched in disgust and spat it out. "We'll have no more of that," she snapped, pointing a turquoise nail at the heart, which dissolved into the waiting earth.

Deborah Tyler-Bennett

An Irreverent Memorial to the Red Clyde Four

For Larry Weiss

Thir wir giants on earth in them days, so thir wir,
Great huge men like McLean, who cud lift
A dockers' strike in wan han, thi other
Cho'in a capitalist.

Or wee Jimmy Maxton, him
Who wis a teacher, screivin his biography u Lenin.
Gallagher wis no bad either, hoddin a commie seat
Way intae the fifties.

But ma favourite wis Kirkwood:
See his autobiography – photae a him getting
        his heid bustid
By the polis in George Square, an the introduction
Written by Winston Churchill. Magic! Way tae go.

Robin Hamilton

The Blackness

Like a discoloured bee, Dad would come home,
grinding coke into the carpets

inking the wall, printing his armchair,
his living touching everything not living.

We could never clean Dad's career
from our memory either.

He retired before the pitheads
fell to the block before blood-bayers.

Out of the blue, the black came back:
miner against miner, coal-black mood.

Seconds out in the red and blue corners.

Scargill and Thatcher, ready for the bell.

Every hour, the clock's hands would pull
bulletins from the television.

It was all that silenced the radio.
Nothing silenced Dad's ranting:

his retirement had deprived him
of a bloody good strike, a juicy chance

to pretend he mattered to Thatcher.
Scargill would never know Dad's blind faith.

Sojourning thugs feigned solidarity.
The bloody battle raged through our village

every day – and Dad couldn't join in.
He cursed the police ("Thatcher's army")

and Mum plied them with tea. They gave her
a silver whistle. Mum blew it in Dad's face

as he blared night into day.
We ceased to exist.

The radio led the funeral march
for a sinking community.

Scargill was king and Adonis
to Dad, in his still-grimed armchair.

Radcliff Gregory

The Customs of the People are Vain

By the time Tanya broached the subject of Christmas, Paul had already agreed to stop going to church, to destroy his ATM card, and to give up pork. He had also built extra shelves in the pantry to store canned goods, beef jerky, water purification tablets, and protein supplements. He had even bought Tanya a shortwave radio so she could listen to James Lloyd's prophecies, broadcast from Oregon, and asked in return only that she not listen while he was at home.

Tanya felt that of all the changes, giving up bacon was the hardest for him. For a while she cooked him some in a separate little frying pan as she made pancakes for the family's Sunday breakfasts. But she would not let him give any to the children, even though their oldest loved bacon. "Bac-, Daddy, bac-!" Stevie would plead, and his cries would crescendo into a long, high-pitched whine. Paul couldn't bear it. "How can you stand this?" he snapped at her.

After that he stopped eating bacon entirely and eventually gave up Sunday breakfasts altogether. He said if they weren't going to church anymore he might as well spend the extra time at the building site.

Tanya knew she had already asked a lot of Paul. She knew he just wanted to live a simple life, to believe what he'd always been taught was right, and to provide for his family. But she felt he had overreacted when Stevie cried about the bacon. Stevie was two, and shrill whining had become his stock response to all unpleasant things: naps, grocery shopping, juice spilled on his socks. So Tanya was mostly immune to his shrieking, but not to his other alarm sounds: she recalled those nights in early September when Stevie had bronchitis, how she sat up with him, rocking him gently and agonizing over each scratchy, bubbling cough, while Paul lay in bed sleeping.

Several weeks after Paul gave up bacon, Tanya brought up the Christmas issue. It was a windy night in mid-November. She and Paul had bathed the children together early in the evening and dressed them in freshly laundered winter pajamas, the plush ones with feet. Paul held Stevie in his lap and told him stories. Tanya rocked William to sleep singing him little songs she'd made up. After they put the children to bed they sat in front of the woodstove in drowsy silence. They could hear the wind howl. Tanya was drifting off to sleep when Paul said: "This is it."

He was half-asleep himself, but he seemed to wake up more as he explained: "This is it. This." And he nodded toward the woodstove and the boys' bedroom. "This is all I ever wanted: my boys sleeping peacefully. The smell of the fire. Listening to the wind outside. Us, safe."

Tanya loved him deeply at that moment.

She knew that Paul believed safety, peace and a warm house were all things they could hold on to as long as they worked hard enough. But Tanya also sensed in Paul a deep feeling of fear. She suspected this meant he knew what she knew, even as he denied it: that the end times were coming, that the tribulation was at hand, that only those who were spiritually and materially prepared, who had studied the scriptures, who had learned God's will, who had listened to the true prophecies would be called the Lord's beloved. She looked at Paul and saw his fear, and recognized it as the fear that came from denial.

"I don't think we should celebrate Christmas this year," she said.

Paul leaned back in his armchair and put his feet on the coffee table. "You don't believe in Jesus anymore?" he said.

She told him she believed in Jesus but December 25 was not Jesus's birthday. Instead it was the day that in ancient Babylon the Sumerians celebrated their god, Tammuz. One of their rituals on that day was to cut down an evergreen tree, bring it inside, and decorate it. God found all this displeasing, as it says in Jeremiah 10: "Learn not the way of the heathen... for the customs of the people are vain: for one cutteth a tree out of the forest... they deck it with silver and with gold; they fasten it with nails and with hammers, that it move not." She said people for all these years had been fooled into thinking that they were celebrating Jesus's birth and pleasing God when all this time they were repeating the rituals of a pagan festival and making God angry.

Paul took his feet off the coffee table.

Tanya was silent, waited.

"William won't know the difference," he said, "he's too little. Stevie won't even notice if we don't make a big deal out of it. But I'm not gonna hang around the house on Christmas Day if we're not doing anything. I'm going to the building site."

Tanya nodded at each point in Paul's litany of considerations.

"You have to tell my mother," he said. "I'm not telling her."

She nodded again. This is how it had been ever since she'd learned the true prophecy. Every aspect of their salvation had to be negotiated, like items in a divorce settlement.

Jodie Clark

Moth Screams

All night they heard the moth
and, with the moth,
the ticking of the clock,
the planes that flew upon their nightly path,
the scratching in the loft of claws on wood,
the hedgehog's click,
the sudden screams of cat.

None of this had troubled sleep before.
Those piercing screams
had not kept them awake.
The rape cry of the vixen come on heat
was natural,
the screeching owl,
a friend.

But words invoked the furies from the ground
and wind threw up a blast upon the house.
The rain, the driving rain, grew fast and loud
and drove its bullets on the groaning house.
They did not sleep.

All night they lay awake within their beds
where words had flown
on moth wings from her mouth.
The creaking house repeated all the words
that echoed back,
from East, West, North and South.

They did not speak.

The kamikaze words flew on all night
around them and the light inside the hall.
Their children found no comfort there that night,
they found no comfort for them there at all,
they could not sleep.
Those moth wings burnt her words upon the night.
She wished each syllable could be unsaid
but on they fluttered, fluttered into light
and flew around each restless, sleepless head,

"None shall sleep now.
None shall sleep now.
Now, none shall sleep," they said.

When, in dawn's light, she rose to change her clothes
she cried to see the damage that was done:
the backless, sexy jumper when they met,
the Aran she had worn as dressing gown,
the neglige in amber tones and jet,
the tiny, white embroidered christening gown,
the black chiffon, the tracksuit for the park;
her life, in clothes, lay ruined in the dark.

Each garment showed the fretting of the moth,
        where
words had eaten memories.
She did not know that words could fly like moths,
"I did not know," she said.

Julie Boden

Seagull Address

Seagulls of the city, hear me.
You peck the way of rubbish grounds,
soar the wind of towers.

Remembering our Fathers you ask me,
"Is it time to take the salt trail back
into our own homeland?"

Look into the twilight, sisters.
Look into the twilight, brothers.
Twilight fools our human brethren too.

See their metamorphosis to moles
who dig the nightfall of these city streets,
who sift the cerebellum of the loam.

Their minds remember those un-blighted lands
as they drop crisp bag, chip bag offerings
appeasing strange potato pasts that haunt them.

"What if we forget?" I hear you say.
"What if we forget the way our ancestors
could fast dive down into the fields of foam?"

And then you come to show these city roofs
where clouds drown in the dusk of their reflections
calling to their birthing place of sea.

Seagulls of the City, I hear you cry,
"Who knows where home is anymore?"

But as you cry you fly upon the wind

and as you fly it seems, at least to me,
that you are quite at home
in city sky.

Julie Boden

(A poem from the exhibition Digbeth to
Eastside *poems by David Hart and Julie
Boden, photography by Richard Green).*

The Coast of Greenland

I'd like to think in blocks. Like a stone man
dreaming of citadels of basalt
or unshattered statements of slate.
Then could I heave

history out of its flow
its cat that slips by the eye
of the watch left out at night.
                    ~
The cat might be a merchant,
a beggar an emissary a thief
or none of the above. Might be
nothing at all

to do with you. Like necessity
that walks by itself. Or water:
alien, healing, fatal.

                ~

I lay me down in the thin stream
its almost visible its
not quite can touch its quick blur
and creatures of change

and thought of Burgess Shale
and an old grey stone
as weathered as a molar

or a mountain in Scotland
stroked by the nimble
boldshy motions:

air, water, dream.

David Bircumshaw

3: WORDS FOR SHOUTING

And, constant voice, protest against the
    wrong …

William Wordsworth, 'On the Projected
    Kendal and Windermere Railway'

Unferth and Beowulf's Monster Flyting

Vaguely after BEOWULF ll. 449-528

The big yin got tae Heorot, nae problem:
"Ahm here fur the monster rammy, but."

"Aye," grunted Unferth intae his beard,
"Aw we bloody need.
        Soddin mental that yin.
                Thinks he's a hard man:
Aw haw, aw the way frae Brigton."

"So," said Unferth, "come tae deal wi thon
        Grendel bummer, huv yi?"

"Hear yi hid a match wi that Brecca,
        swimming or something?"

"Aye," smarmed Beowulf, buffin his nails
        oan his jacket lapels,
"No a bad show, that."

So Unferth spoke
        (pittin the semantic heid oan Wulfy):

"See you, yi couldnae swim
        across a puddle in ra fog."

Thus Unferth continued:

"Daft as brushes, the pair aw yi,
        drookit fur a week staunin unner the shower
                in the weans' changin room –
Nearest yi ever gote tae the sea."

"And onywey, Brecca licked the breeks affy yi."

"Youz pair couldnae even
        sook a sherbert dab
                tae save yir lives."

"Yir a right sad bastard,
        an if yi hing aroon the Hall
                the night, waiting fur Grendel,
Ahl believe it when Ah bite it."

"Widnae cross the road
        Tae spit oan yir grave."

There wiz Beowulf, face like a midden,
        glowrin somethin awfu –
                till he came back wi a pit-doon:
"Despite yir gallus tongue, Unferth, yir damned."

"AN yir pissed oot o yir skull,
        yi illiterate wee shite."

Then Beowulf spoke:

"See us a pint u heavy, jimmy,
        an Ahl tell youz
                how it *really* wiz … "

TAE BE CONTINUED

Robin Hamilton

Tomboys

Some women used to be tomboys. Even now they like to ride, not push, the supermarket cart. Run, hop, whoosh. They like to race workday commuters; they rev their engines at red lights, nod to the driver who sports a perplexed expression in the next lane, and when the light turns green, they speed away. These women are never squeamish; they don't mind what the cat drags in because death is always fascinating. One thing they don't like though is a humdrum life, so sometimes they toss it all to climb a tree and refuse to come down.

A woman has just tossed it all and climbed a tree. Her name is June and she's not coming down. She sits high in the magnolia, one of many that line the street. It is spring and the trees are in full bloom. It is a sweet smelling time, shaded and green, a lovely place to live. June picks the creamy white flowers and tosses them on the head of the dog that's yapping at the trunk trying to climb up after her.

June's boy, Jack, jumps up and down, "Look," he says to his sister, "Mom's stuck in a tree."

"Au contraire, mon frère; I've never been stuck," June says, "I'm a tree-climbing specialist, the best."

The girl, Melody, her youngest, informs June that this isn't what mothers do. They do not climb trees and she should know better. Melody knows this despite the fact that she scored high on the Pre-School activities Inventory because she was selected to participate in a very special reorientation class at school for a select group of high-scoring girls with similar dispositions.

June's husband, Bill, sees his wife's tan muscular leg swinging back and forth, a sporty sexy pendulum, and wishes someone had warned him about women who used to be tomboys when they were girls, and how they didn't make good wives.

Neighbors frown from their doorways and walkways. They don't like it when a grown woman climbs a tree; she's a woman, not a boy, they think. They are not happy, and they hope that the woman in the tree understands this; they sigh loudly just in case. It could be, they fear, a trend – worse yet, a crisis. Just last week in fact, Hilary Sandoval jumped off her roof onto a trampoline while her kids were at school. She even somersaulted in the air. It had gone on for hours; it was unseemly. The husbands learned about it from their wives when they came home from their jobs that evening. They agreed that a woman somersaulting off her roof onto a trampoline in the middle of the day was indecent, and should be stopped. At night, though, the husbands remembered how Hilary used to beat them at everything when they were boys and she was a girl, and they fell asleep and dreamed of Hilary tumbling head over heals, the lycra of her Nike running pants hugging her athletic form, emphasizing her strong legs, her gym-trained hamstrings and quadriceps. The men moaned in their sleep, Oh those thewy thighs.

One woman in an Emily Bryant pantsuit would like to talk some sense into the woman in the tree but remembers June from school many years before and is afraid June will say something inappropriate and embarrass her in front of the neighbors.

Another woman stands on her porch with flour-powdered hands; she is wearing a red, white, and blue apron with the words, *One Nation Under Mom.* She suspects June's behaviour is a result of prenatal PCB exposure; June's mother, Mae, dead three years from cancer, bless her, probably ate contaminated fish while gallivanting in the woods at one of those braless retreats during the seventies. That whole lot of mannish women had peopled the town with loud-mouthed dirt-faced girls, who grew up without boundaries; the consequences were incidents like these, the woman was sure. She watches as June taunts the onlookers with a chin up on a high and not so sturdy looking branch, and thinks June is looking a tad broad-shouldered, probably from knocking elbows with men in the weight room at the Y. She reminds herself to write June a note suggesting she take up a more elongating exercise like Pilates.

June swings herself up like a gymnast, locks her legs around a branch, and hangs upside down. Emily Bryant and One Nation Under Mom exchange looks with one another. They think June is wearing shorts too short and her shirt is sliding a little too high for the eyes of kids and men. It could be worse, they tell themselves; she could be pretty. Fortunately, they sigh in relief, June is more brawn that beaut. Nevertheless, they are happy their husbands are at work; men are unpredictable; who knows what they like.

A man stands nearby and smokes a pipe. He's on his daily walkabout for the neighbourhood association; he's its eyes and ears he likes to say. He volunteered for the job. Let me be the eyes and ears, he had said. The association members said sure, and he went out and bought a pipe. He inspects June's husband and children, and thinks, That man does not have the upper hand and, Those children will grow up to be a menace, the types who cross the street when the sign clearly says Don't Walk. The man dislikes people like this and can't help but glare at the children, future thorns in his side. He tries to focus on the family to avoid looking at June but like a moth to flame his eyes are drawn to her sinewy arms and her right bulging bicep – a protruding reminder of his defeat. In the seventh grade, she dared him to arm-wrestle for his lunch. She liked what he had, she said, she liked Hostess Snowballs. And for those sugary-processed treats his mother packed for him special, she pinned his puny arm to the table, humiliating him in front of a cafeteria full of taunting school-chums. And when he cried she said, Don't be a baby, and ate his lunch. All these years later, he still does not want to draw her attention, and so he slowly backs away.

June sees the man who slowly backs away and calls, "Hiya, Bob, remember me?"

Of course he did. No matter how hard he tried, he could never forget. He tells June he is an informant for the N.A., its eyes and ears, and how does she like that? June, who still hangs by her legs, puts her hands behind her head and pulls herself up with an abdominal crunch. She picks a magnolia, and tosses it on his head. Climb on up, she says. We can arm-wrestle.

The man hurries away, ignoring June's chicken sounds that fill his ears, to where the neighbors are gathering on One Nation Under Mom's porch. What shall we do they ask one another.

An old Russian man says, "Clearly the woman needs to be romanced. Maybe a young man can play a song on his guitar – no, ukulele! – and melt her icy heart. She will fall in love and climb down into his arms, a quivering, blushing mass of woman."

This is no fairytale, the neighbors say to the Russian; this is the suburbs. We don't know what you do in your backyard, but in this neighborhood, we have rules. The Russian reminds them that he's been their neighbour for years, and they think, If proximity a neighbour make, we'd have no problems.

The neighbors all agree, however, that they can't stand idly by while a grown woman threatens the order of things, the good manners of good living. They decide that these events will only escalate if they don't put a stop to it. From now on, they decide, they will nip this activity in the bud. They will start with June. Only none of them wants to confront her. Who knows what she might do, they say. They decide to call the fire department. It is a unanimous decision.

They hear the siren sound and the neighbors think, Finally we are rescued. The red engine arrives and the captain hops out and looks up at June.

"That ain't a kitten," the captain says, running her hand through her crew cut. "Call us when you have a real emergency." The captain puts her helmet back on, climbs onto the engine where Amber, Billie, and Brenda await, and together they speed away.

The neighbors are taken aback. When did we get an all-female fire department? They ask. When did men stop saving women? They suspect this is more than a crisis, they fear they are doomed. The boisterous, bold, and fearless girls had not been taken out in their teens, as they assumed, but had grown up and taken over. How did this happen, the neighbors wonder? When did we lose control?

These days someone says they hear June is an aerobatic wing-walker, or some such. They say they don't care for women who used to be tomboys when they were girls. Look at them, much too confident, sunbathing half-naked; running around like the neighbourhood's a beach. Too big, they are, too physical, they like the sound of their voices too much. Listen; there goes the neighbourhood

Mystie Hood

Po[st]face[d]

Wir aw intae that
    Wordsworth Rap
      the day

– but what *iz* the real
    langiwig o men?

Ah mean, no very
    poliically correc but

Whit wid be the Reel

"language" o wimin?

Coupla wifies havin a
        crack in the close?

Scream uf rage at the
        glass ceilin?

Cut yir baws aff
        sooniz lookit yi.

                                    Robin Hamilton

Powerful Emotions Simulated

Life on the left – reality on the right:

Press start, select your team,
Red tops, white shorts and socks,
Embrace the joy-pad controller,
Playing with triangles, thrusting squares,
And caressing circles.
Revolving the analogue like a magic wand,
Enchanting twenty-two digital creatures.
Glaring green grass, growing
Powerful pixels in our minds.
Artificial bodies flickering,
Fingers tapping frantically,
tap, tap, tap.
Pass and move, through ball,

Jump, dash, goal flash, across
The world within the window, while
Ultraviolet eyes light up the screen.

Header, tackle, pass and shoot,
A striker fires his rifle,
The bullet slices through virtual air,
The keeper bomb-diving like a falcon,
Missing the flock – and it's there,
A GOAL! Unreal crowd chanting,
Replaying the image again and again,
Copies of copies of,
Colours flashing on the screen.
Stoppage time, minutes to go,
Dirty tackle, calling for a PENALTY!
Shouting, swearing, hands in the air,
Scarlet faces with false despair.
The man in black calls for time,
Like the grim reaper he seals our fate,
Now back to reality, time to awake.

Leigh Chia

Adolescent Rhubarb Stalks the Muse

"I wandered lonely as a clod."

For SJD

Ahm no jist a
    n egoistical
        Perpendicular Pronoun

        see me, ahm sumbodi –

bit whit yi might caw
    "a locus of perception"

Ahm eye

Robin Hamilton

Taurus (May 1918-2000)

Imagine a raging bull ....
    Foam and spittle dripping from mouth
    and nostrils,
    Fast, hot breath,
    The keen eye set steady for retribution.
    He roars. He bellows.
    He charges towards his goal:

The earth will tremble
　　Tears will fall
　　Limbs will shake
　　When all at once –

　　He stops.
　　And slowly
Lowers
　　His
　　Heavy
　　Head
　　To examine the tiny veins,
　　On the petals of a flower,
　　Lit up by the sun.

　　I'll miss you, Tom.

Susan Bell

Little Concert of Readers' Letters

In answer to your previous I wish to complain
to point out the question the problem that lies
in the beginning of time in Horsham last Thursday
from Bolton by Barnsley near Arroyo de la Miel
at Grand Falls St Helier that's Cambridge Berks
from the friends of abolition the voices of time
the unsigned sincerely our standards yours truly
in anger in sadness off Livingstone Road
as an answer to your previous the point of it all
to anyone who listens when molecules vibrate

because of the footprints the forensic reports
at the End of the Universe on a Llangollen bus
embalming a pharoah the first time I saw her
like Minoan script the flight of the bees
a Last Chance Café the Guides as we call them
on a pensioner's takehome the powers to be
in puzzlement in Frankfurt by the edge of the dawn
as an owl called Prime Minister when last the full moon
in the mists of our origins the phone calls began
with problems like mine so botanists explain
began with the Government's the Empire's decline
an oil price crescendo the crisis of faith
our hopes for the futons the right of free speech
concerning your previous the Editor's voice
I would like to complain I wish to protest
as dusk falls on Rotherham the sound of violins
the answer to the problem the point of it all
a philosopher's stone or costing the Ferryman
the Armies of Metaphysics the boatloads of Verse
the madness of rivers the babbling of the day
on the banks of oblivion we wish to maintain

David Bircumshaw

4: WORDS FOR SINGING

The thrush-cock sings, bright, irrelevant
things ...

- Edward Thomas, 'Roads '

Roundabout

Corrugated Castles line streets and shops
Sell single hubcaps found in sewers, where
A small boy floats his boats made from flip-flops.
Dry dust suffocates and stench hits the air.
Battered engines squeal, mates shout, horns prevail,
Around rutted roads, traffic six lanes wide.
Island life. Mothers selling water fail
To feel burning sun, there so long. With pride
They work to feed children babies, who sleep on
Their backs, unconscious, as near-missed danger
Sails by. Young chancers watch, then prey on
Circumnavigating crowds, a stranger
To this world stops, not wanting to disturb,
And views the children's playground from the curb.

Vicky Smith

*(A mate is a young boy who works on
African tro-tros, which are old minibuses
used for public transport. His job is to
take the money and hang out of the
window calling out his route repeatedly to
those who wait on the side of the road).*

Suitable for Vegetarians

(Bold syllables emphasised to make rhythmic chant).

I don't **want** to hunt a **deer**
I don't **want** to catch a **fish**
My **chant** or **charm** or **spell**'s for
A **nice** vege**tar**ian **dish**.

I don't **want** to eat **quorn**
I don't **want** to eat **soy**a
But **if** it's pre**sent**ed I'll **eat it**:
I **don't** want to **be** an ann**oy**er.

So... **brocc**oli, **cel**ery, **beans**,
Spinach and **all** other **greens**
Vegetables **come** to my **hob** – no de**lay**!
I'll be **gobb**lin' a **charm**ing **meal** up to**day**!

Kate Sharp

Future Pathway

You asked me to write about you
You said I never had
I promised I'd try
Say sorry for anything blue we have

Rocking to-fro to-fro
Baby in my arms
Dreams, visions, bitter tastes of a fire place
Demons danced away
Your divine arms

Sometimes I find it hard to say
What I see
Catphrases often take shelter from me.
Each morning I stare at you when awake
Creep out like red Santa
St Nic on a shimmering morning.
I never want to leave!
Head over heart

Rocking to-fro to-fro
Baby in my arms
Dreams, visions, sour tastes of a fire place
Demons danced away
Your divine arms

I know that sometimes I leave
Sometimes you feel white
Sometimes I bet you sit there
Feeling distant, grey, alone.

Rocking to-fro to-fro
Baby in my arms
Dreams, visions, salt tastes of a fire place
Demons danced away
Your divine arms

Mouths, lips, and bodies taste divine
Sometimes silent, we sit and stare
While having conversations of life and love, while

Rocking to-fro to-fro
Baby in my arms
Dreams, visions, and sweet tastes of a fire place
Demons danced away
Your divine arms

The future is not yet known.
Every morning for the next lifetime I don't want
        to leave the room
Hate imagining you alone.
May the taste linger on
And the conversation remain in our heads as one.

Robin Webber-Jones

5: WORDS FOR PERFORMING

And after me, a strange tide turns …

- Wilfred Owen, 'Shadwell Stair'

De worthiness of Argument

*(A little argument spices up luv
And life now and then)*

Widout women,
Dere would be no men.
Widout men,
Dere would be no women.
Widout women and men,
Dere would be no argument.
An' widout de spice of argument,
De world would be seasonless an' full of zombies.

Gabriel Eshun

What the Baobab Saw .... The Groundnut Scheme

*(Reading instruction: Assume the deep,
slow voice of a wise four hundred year-
old African Baobab tree).*

1947, I remember
white men
they did come:
In the form of

military operation.
Plant their seeds
oil from the farm.

Canvas town.
Work began.
New mechanised
Agriculture.
Clear 100,000 acre.
They said;
Technology
The future.

Bush so strong
no rhino
only snake
is passing through.
Underestimated
jungle, scrub
impenetrable.

Women came
with babies,
doctors, priests,
built homes.
Some ground clear
Peanuts planted
No rains came.

No rains came.
In fertile soil
plants grow.
Celebration
Rains came,
Clay soil sets
Harvest impossible.

No oil made
Home shortage,
Millions lost
No gain.
Nature
would not let them
have their way.

In the shade
of this Baobab
they discuss
their blunder.
This great continent,
gave no further.

1961, Independence.

Vicky Smith

(Tanganyika (now known as Tanzania)
received independence in 1961. The
majority of the Groundnut Scheme took
place there).

The Paget Arms

It's a time warp this place, a black hole.
In here time is lost.
There's no clock on the wall to prompt movement,
no hands to direct you home.
Your dinner sits cold on a cracking plate, as the
lonely pace the floor, awaiting the beer-breath kiss
and clumsy grope goodnight.

It's like the land that time forgot, this place.
Fossils from a prehistoric age,
embalm themselves in pints of amber nectar.
Like caged rodents they sniff around,
searching for boredom breakers.
Their nicotine fingers lay to rest in the
venomous brimming trays. They chew
on fatty rinds and wish they were somewhere else.

It's like a drug, this place.
Imprisoned in its four walls, they grope
for wooden cues – the emblem of 'the man'.
The mossy table is their grave.

Hours disappear as they
smack shiny balls into darkened pockets,
praying for the glory of victory.
In here, they can be champions.
The walls, colour of cancer, bear scars of a
thousand misjudged battles.
Ale soldiers blindly throw their mini spears,
missing the enemy one by one.
Wounded, they stumble back to
the wooden pews, seeking solace in toxic optics.

It smells like a coffin, this place.
Crumbling skeletons of the glory years line
the dusty shelves and lurk in cobwebbed corners.
A stuffed trout, its glassy eyes staring,
watches over its hapless congregation.
Tug Wilson and Herbert Slade pose, fists clenched,
ready to fight their way out of their glass prisons.
But, they too are trapped in this black magic place.
Paget, frozen in time, stares out from his
        wooden frame.
His Mecca now a breeding ground for disease.

It's a time warp, this place.

A black hole.

Mellissa Flowerdew-Clarke

Public Toilets

Some people love going into public toilets,
They are proud to make other visitors listen to their
Plops, dribbles, streams and farts.
They have no shame about their natural bodily
        functions,
They gain satisfaction when "shitting on
company time."

Other people are not so brash.
They hold in their excrement,
Inflicting upon themselves hours of stomach cramps,
Squeezing their tightened bowels.
Some extreme cases of shyness
Results in minutes wasted of lunch hours,
Waiting for every last person to vacate the premises,
Before the dreaded act can be done.

There is a certain public toilet etiquette,
As with everything,
If you get it wrong, prepare for a black mark on
        your public report.
You can smile a little at others,
But do *not* make eye contact when you've just
        listened to them
Rustling their sanitary towel into the bin provided.

Maybe your personal response to public toilets says
A lot about your character.
Those who can't, are inverted,
Those who can, loudly, are extroverted.

Or maybe a bad experience can shun the most
    confident person
Into the shadows of shame,
Backing them into a life of
Holding it all in.

Louise Pymer

My Old Lie Café

Just round the corner
Down 80s way
A bustle of lifeless life
Inside the Old Lie Café
There weren't many people left
Round the shadowy white camel hair
Cloths check red on table tops
Smell of burnt Arabic coffee,
Forgotten
Again
And the taste of sweet dust
In the air the dim glow from tiny
Lanterns whispered in reply
To the radio
I could hear playing
'Coronation on a Phoenician Shrine'
looooo looooo loooooooooooooooo
Tahir and Hassan at the bar sat
Drunk on sour date wine
Distorted Black Laurel and Hardy

Replicas come to life.
Osman just lay there cried himself dumb
numb head swung down
Young Jackob on a rusty wheelchair
Squeaked his way to the bar
Squeeeak squeeak squeak
Loooooooooo looooooo loooooooooooo
I saw Grandpa Adam poring over his maps
Cup held quivering peering over
Monocle and magnifying glass
Searching over splashes and splodges,
Smudges of corpses left on the isle down south.
On his right sat a young couple,
The lady dragged on her Marlboro Lights
Her auburn braided hair sprang up on end
Like sparrow's nest after a deadly lovers' fight
Mr. Macho seemed bored witless,
With an empty gaze over her head he looks and looks
and looks

*(Poem based on a painting by John Keane
(1989)).*

Maha Mahmoud

Liminal Incident

Ah wiz walkin doon
      Sauchiehall Street
when this big fuckin
      ostridge
accosted me
      sellin copies o
      the Big Issue.

"Wawn u copie, Jimmy?"
it said.

"No thank you, my man,"
    I retorted.
"Bought it in Edinburgh yesterday."

Robin Hamilton

Cosmetic Surgery

It's a simple modern wonder,
just slip your dollars under their mat
become the new you,
and embrace a better life.
Because the old one frankly, a joke,
was no good whatsoever.

You can buy yourself a painted smile.
You can wear a dress threaded with a million lies.

You can get new skin and eyes.
Shine your plastic teeth,
from the tight mouth of a face,
carved with clinical precision
by a white-washed surgeon.
The stabs and tears of the knife,
adding back the life – *excitement*,
to your mortal body

And how they want excitement!
Faceless hoards picking a face,
from a flickering computer screen,
'It'll knock twenty years off of you',
they say.
That blade, that dripping blood
flesh of butter falling away,
      with the doomed marriage,
         the family rows,
            his affair with that girl,
the years of spiritual decay,
the dull, relentless Sunday afternoons
where a woman stared in silence at a man,
and wished the earth would claim her dying body,

the old body,
weathered and worn ,
its sagging lines and lumps of flabby flesh
in the bin with the medical waste,
its honesty polluting the new you,

It was a telling body,
a face which betrayed secret tears
a lined mouth that told the truth,
with every half-hearted smile.

It was a novel,
a poem,
a song.
It was a book of hushed stories,
perhaps featuring a heroine
with a laugh as fresh as morning,
a smile like a wildflower,

and quite frankly it was no good whatsoever.

Maria D. Orthodoxou

Perfect History

The Greatest Briton,
The Nation's pride,
Is this a perfect history?
Digging for victory,
So vital to find,
Sounds like ignorant bliss to me.

Never was so much,
Known to so few,
Is this a perfect history?
About our hero,
Our bulldog tattoo.
Sounds like ignorant bliss to me.

Is this a perfect
Is this a perfect
Is this a perfect
Is this a perfect
History? History?

Rescued our country,
From the Blitzkrieg,
Suicide in Gallipoli,
Man of the people,
With Stalin in league,
'Commy' strikes killed by military

Our finest hour,
We made Europe free,
H-Bombs became necessary,
Kingdom United,
Parties in the street,
Nationalistic legacy.

Is this a perfect
Is this a perfect
Is this a perfect
Is this a perfect
History? History?

Gareth Watts

Elegy for the Admirable

> *(Sir James Crichton (1560-1582): poet,*
> *swordsman, philosopher, lover.*
> *Commemorated by Thomas Urquart in*
> *The Jewel as the Admirable Crichton).*

Ah had that Jimmy Crichton in the back of ma
    cab once –
      mental he was – a right heid case.
Ah said, Whit dyi reckon the odds ur fur the
    next Old Firm game?

But aw he could do was go on and on and on
    about this bird
      forget her name, but …

See, he couldnae get his mind affy hir.

Next time ah had him in ma cab, he wis
deid – stone cold.

Bit o a waste, eh?

Stuck a blanket under him, sae
his corpse widnea drip on the seat.

So much for all those perfect gentle knights.

Robin Hamilton

"He never writes to me no more":

A Story for Children

"He never writes to me no more," she says.

"How can he write to you when he's been dead for fifty years?" I say.

Then she cries a bit.

After a while, she brightens up, and says:

"He never writes to me no more."

And I say:

"How can he write to you when he's been dead for fifty years?"

And she cries again.

"Grandma," I say, "Korea was a long time ago. Grandpa was a long time ago. We've got iPods now. And texting, so you don't need letters."

"Oh," she says, and she's quiet for a bit. The clock tick tock ticks in the corner and I think about the door and tonight's telly. To be honest, this place frightens me. It smells. Down the corridor, someone else's grandma is screaming that goblins are using her toothbrush.

"He never writes to me no more."

"Grandma," I sigh.

My mum says that grandma's got a disease called Alzheimer's which makes her forget. She says it gives her a kind of amnesia, if you know what that is. She says she can't cope with it any more, cos grandma keeps forgetting that grandpa's long dead. We keep having to remind her. And it's news all over again. And she cries for him. And forgets again. And wonders where he is.

It's like grandpa's dying over and over in her head, every few minutes.

But really he died millions of years ago. There was a war in a country called Korea. He was on America's side. He died when they were attacked at Yalu River on the 25th October, 1950. I know all about it, you see. I looked it up. Grandpa died of drowning, they reckoned, and they didn't find his body. One day, his letters to grandma just stopped.

"He never writes to me no more."

Grandma says this and cries, and for the umpteenth time shows me the bundle of brown letters she keeps in a biscuit tin in the corner. Funny, but she never forgets where that is. Personally, I'd prefer it if the letters were biscuits. That's what normal grandmas would give me. Normal grandmas'd pat me on the head, say "ooh, you've grown," and give me grandma-kind of biscuits, like Rich Tea or Digestives. And perhaps a few quid. But no, not my Alzheimer's grandma. I just get smelly old letters.

The letters are the letters grandpa sent her from Korea. The last one, on top, is from the 24th October, 1950. He must've been already dead when she got it – kinda spooky-like, I reckon. It's very short, and he just says: 'Dear Glad, thanks for your letter. Tomorrow's a biggish day. Will write when it's over.

Mosquitoes nasty as ever.' Then there's some blah-blah squishy stuff, and he signs off once and (I suppose) for ever.

"He never writes to me no more."

My mum lost it yesterday when grandma said that for the trillionth time. She burst into tears and said she hated seeing her mum like this. Then she shouted at grandma: "He's dead, don't you get it? Dead dead dead dead dead." I thought the word sounded weird, repeated like that. It goes sort of funny, as if you're not sure what it means any more. But no one else was laughing. Everyone else was shouting and crying at once. Even the hard nurse with the tattoo. And my grandma was in floods cos grandpa had died again.

I didn't know what to do. It was horrid.

So – and I know you'll think it's really weird what I'm going to tell you. But anyway, let's get it over with, and you can think whatever you like.

You see, last night, I sat down and wrote a letter. Never written one before except at school. And not even at school a love letter. They don't teach you that in Year 5.

I'd nicked one of the old letters from the biscuit tin, and I did my best to copy grandpa's ancient style of writing – squiggly 'Ts' and spidery bits. It was dead hard and took ages, I tell you. Then I folded it in an envelope, got a stamp from my mum's purse, and addressed it to grandma in the home. I didn't write 'Grandma' on it – I put 'Mrs Gladys Hailwood' plus the home's address.   Then I shoved it in the pillar box down the street.

Feel free to think I'm weird when you find out what it was about.   Maybe I am.   All I know is that when I went today grandma had stopped saying "He never writes to me no more." Instead, she was smiling in a long-time-ago way, if you know what I mean.   She even offered me a Rich Tea.   Though still no cash.

Anyway, here goes.   What I wrote went like this:

'Dear Glad,

'Hello from Korea. I'm sorry I haven't written you for the last fifty-five years, but I've been a bit caught up with some stuff. You know what wars are like. So sorry about that.

'But here I am again.   Things are cool in Seoul. Wish you were here.

'I just wanted to say that I miss you truck-loads.   You're great and we'll see each other again very soon.

'With love and all that, Frank.'

Jonathan Taylor

Continuing Investigation

It must've been one of the burnt
out cars in the park that rose
to stalk our little girl. Or the oak

along Keeper's Walk, by the pond, charred
at its base, and stabbed
with nails. Maybe

that shopping-trolley in The Brook lashed
out like a rusty net.

Was it some metal figure, buzzing, that burst
from the mains sub-station
at the bottom of Dove Lane? Chased her? Yes,

it must've been an electric touch
made such marks on her.

Perhaps it was the grass grown
long this summer that wrapped
first round her wrists; then

her neck.

Must've been the air, must
've been nothing
that sucked away her voice; pulled
at her, pulled

her away from us. Something
soft & silent & instant & peace .... The police

have their beliefs.

Mark Goodwin

Death Ride

Curtis suspected that the car had something to do with it. As daft as this sounded, he'd felt okay when he'd first pulled off. It seemed, though, that the longer he spent behind the wheel, the more he felt a growing emptiness developing in his mind.

First thing: he had never believed in spooks and ghouls. Second thing: he had always reserved judgement about people who thought that you could steal someone's shadow with a feeling of pity. For Curtis, the line that existed between fantasy and the humdrum world of reality was not just solid; it was as thick as the walls of the Channel Tunnel.

He'd stolen the car after leaving the hotel. In a carefully planned heist, he'd 'taken' over 300 grand from the Outfit in a computer scam. Taking the car was an afterthought. It was just sat there; the keys dangling invitingly from the ignition. *Why not?* Curtis thought. *Sure beats the bus*. In a final two fingered salute, he'd jumped in and driven off. At the time, taking the car seemed such a good idea. That was until three of the Outfit's goons had given chase.

Curtis had driven through the twisty streets of the city without any respect for speed limits. Once he'd reached the outskirts he'd floored the accelerator, quickly leaving the goons' car far behind him.

It was only much later that Curtis began to feel a little strange. Although the car he was driving could hardly be described as a powerful machine, it'd pulled away from the Outfit's henchmen far too quickly for such a model.

But it wasn't just the car's performance that worried Curtis. When he thought about it he couldn't remember the last time he'd stopped for petrol. Two hours? Three hours? Surely not four! The odometer on the dash read that he'd travelled 440 miles; yet the petrol gauge still showed full. That couldn't be right; he couldn't have driven for all that distance without using fuel. Come to think of it, he couldn't have driven all those miles without stopping for a break! He'd only been in the car a short while; hadn't he? The thing was, he just couldn't remember.

The road opened up in front of him, and despite his growing tiredness, Curtis decided to try something. Pushing the accelerator as if he were trying to squeeze it through the floor, he stared in amazement as the needle on the speedometer climbed round the dial. Not possible, it just wasn't possible. A strange queasiness began to settle on Curtis. It made him feel as if he'd been given an electric shock. He started to ease his foot off the accelerator when –

BANG

The sound cracked off like a starting pistol. What was it? Glancing in the mirror, Curtis just managed to see a group of figures behind a crop of bushes pulling something back in across the road: a stinger. They'd used an old police trick to puncture his tyres. The car slewed violently across the road, the ruined tyres shedding chunks of rubber like the skin of some giant black snake. The rear wheels started to break away as Curtis over-corrected the slide, narrowly missing a signpost.

What did they say? Don't brake, use the gears instead? Curtis downshifted, the transmission screaming in protest. Glancing in the mirror once more, he could make out the lights of a car fast approaching.

Curtis wondered how they had managed to get in front of him. He'd left them miles behind. While he knew his destination, he had no fixed idea of the route he was going to take. So how had they been able to lie in wait for him and use the stinger?

Suddenly, the tyres found purchase on the road as if they'd re-inflated. With its new found grip, the car leapt forward and accelerated.

How the hell can tyres re-inflate? Curtis' tired mind protested. It just wasn't possible.

The lights from the car behind him dwindled away until they were nothing more than just faint specs of light in his mirror.

By now Curtis was covered in a cold sweat that was leaving him chilled. While he focused on bringing his ragged breathing under control, he tried lifting his hand from the wheel to ease down through the gears; but couldn't. It felt as if there were lead weights tied to the end of his fingers.   He tried breaking, but quickly found that the same happened with his feet.

A smell started to fill the car.   Curtis panicked, thinking it may be exhaust fumes. He'd read an article once where a serial killer had redirected the exhaust pipes into the rear of his taxi. With the glass partition, the driver was relatively safe, but his passengers would end up suffocating to death from the carbon monoxide.

Under the smells of plastic and lemon freshener,   Curtis   could   definitely   smell something.   When he concentrated, it didn't smell so much like exhaust fumes, but rotting rubbish.

The strange itching that had first started in his hands had now escalated into an intense burning; it felt as if all the skin were flaking off underneath the black leather gloves he was wearing. Risking a glance in the mirror, Curtis was sickened by what he saw. Rather than the face he'd known all his life, the one that stared back at him was old and ravaged. It looked like the face of a 95 year-old; and it was ageing fast.   It was as if the car were sucking his life away to generate its supernatural energy.

I'm choking! Curtis thought to himself, and what came out was something croaky and faint. He tried to claw at his throat, but he still couldn't take his hands off the wheel. He tried turning it, but it was as if the car had a mind of its own.   He could feel his heart hammering alarmingly inside his ribs. How much more of this could it stand? He tried to scream out loud, but he had no breath.

He glanced down at the illuminated dials on the dashboard. The circular dials of the speedometer and rev counter appeared like eyes to Curtis. In his heightened state of panic he thought that one winked at him.

Of course he knew what was happening. It was the car; it was its way of getting rid of him for ridiculing the Outfit's boss, Jimmy Fats, the Big Daddy himself. The rumours that Jimmy was into black magic must be true; he'd had the car possessed. Such ravings were that of a mad man, Curtis knew, but he was prepared to accept anything.

His throat felt raw and cracked, he tried gasping for more air but his strength was too weak. His clothes hung on his skeletal frame as if he were nothing more than a bag of bones. He had the idea that if he could only get out of the car, everything would work out right.

In a final bid for survival, Curtis threw what little strength he had left in trying to turn the steering wheel. As if giving him one last chance, the car seemed to help him. It swerved off the road, crashing through a metal gate. Lurching over the rough bumpy ground, the front off-side wheel crashed violently down into a deep, water filled hole. The car bounced free with a bone jarring jolt, only to smash into a tree.

Later, as the engine quietly ticked itself cool, a figure in a long black coat and fedora approached the car. Using an iron bar that he'd been carrying, the newcomer prised open the driver's door with a shriek of metal. As the figure pushed its head into the car, the smell of rotting rubbish intensified.

"Don't feel so clever now, do you?" the figure hissed, its breath pluming out into the chill air of the car's interior.

As Curtis slipped into death, the strange figure in the black coat was the only witness as the car slowly began to de-crumple and straighten back out. Within minutes it looked as if it'd come straight from the showroom.

Sucking the last bits of energy from Curtis' tired body like a metal leach, all that was left was a pile of dust, some dirty rags on the driver's seat and two black leather gloves that lay atop a scuffed pair of work boots.

The dark figure swept them away and started the engine. Reversing the car, he joined his companions who were waiting for him back at the twisted ruin of the smashed gate. With a silent nod of acknowledgement, the other figures climbed back into their car and headed off.

The dark figure glanced back one final time into the field, before the electric window wound up with a soft whine. The moon reflected off the glass, turning it opaque, and obscuring his twisted smile.

Nathan Vaughan

In Black and White

In black and white …

I need it in black and white.
Stating to and from.
What, where, when and why.

Not in hieroglyphics
That I can't understand,
Or in foreign language –
I don't like French,
It may be pretty
But I'm not, I'm English.

Come to think of it,
Don't type it either,
In some solid font
Reproduced from whirring machine
(Liable to crash)
indifferent and staring at me
From the ugly glare
Of pristine paper.

I want it crumpled,
With a coffee mark ring,
Chocolate smear,
Crumbs falling out of the envelope
(Preferably big ones, for me to nibble)

Or, dramatic,
Blood stained,

Tear stained,
Semen stained
(If it's that kind of letter)

In handwriting,
Not your lady-friend's swirly lettering
But yours:
Scribbled, smudged biro,
Scruffy.
Unreadable, almost.
No need for sentences.
Words will do.
I'll know what you mean.
First class stamp please,
Oh,
And lick the envelope.

Victoria Rose Poolman

Happy Families:
A Monologue

You'll never guess what? *(Pause)* Wassatt?
Yes, go on then. I'm pouring myself a glass too.
Kids in bed? Mine too. Knocked them out with
some cough medicine. Wassatt? No, perfect
health thanks. No, no colds. Anyway, with all
that Night Nurse running through their veins
they should sleep through.
　　　Smoking? No, given up. You too?
Marvellous. Don't want my kids having to grow

up without a mother.

Wait there. Just going to get my lighter.
Yes, just the one with a nice glass of wine. Be
like old times. Only we're on the end of a
phone.

(Pause) Oh bedlam. Been playing me up
rotten all day. Whingeing and scrapping from
the moment they got up. Six o'clock it was this
morning. By breakfast I was at my wit's end.
I'd been through my "making collages out of
milk bottles, castles out of old sheets and
drawing mummy a picture" routine.

Took them off to the shops.

Samantha said "fuck" in Tesco's. I was in
the queue and she asked me for some Smarties.
I told her 'smartly' she could think again. I'd
already caught her munching her way through a
packet of Chewits she got from the treat drawer
after breakfast. I told her if she ate any more
sweets her teeth would fall out. Considering she
is still on her first set, it would be a shame.

Anyway, she looks at me, bright as a
button, all blonde curls and big blue eyes, and
says in a voice as clear as a whistle. "Fuck's
sake, mum." Can you believe it? Five years
old! I nearly died right then and there. I said
"what did you say?" hoping to God nobody had
heard. And she repeated it. Louder. "Fuck's
sake, mum."
The looks I got in that queue. If you could still
belt kids without being arrested, I'd have
whipped her backside so hard she wouldn't have
seen next week.

No. Don't know where she got it from. I don't allow swearing in my house. Anyway I put them both in the crèche for the afternoon. A new one. At the Leisure Centre. You can have a facial and get your nails done and the kids can amuse themselves. The carers look barely out of nappies, but it gives me some space. Roy? Oh same as ever. Still hasn't finished the arbour. You know, my shady retreat at the bottom of the garden. He started it at Easter and the kids are going back to school next week. Six months it's taken him to put up one side. I said to him it'll be winter soon and you've got another thing coming if you think I'm sitting shivering, cold and wet in that thing. The wood doesn't even match the colour of the fence. God knows what the neighbours think. And he's missed so many days out with the kids while he's been tinkering with it. Thinks he's Michael bloody Angelo.

Our holiday? Oh lovely, thanks. Drove to France, place near Brittany. Took us two days to get there. Henry threw Roy's prized CD collection out of the window. Five hundred pounds worth of his priceless CDs. Gone. We were on the motorway but had to turn back. By the time we charged back to the spot, they'd vanished. Between you and I, I'm surprised anyone wanted to nick them. Rock from a hundred years ago, some slushy new romantic pop and some maudlin tripe by some bloke called Nick Rave. Doesn't sound as if he's ever been to a rave to me. *(Giggles).* Course I

remember those days. Innocence and freedom.
Until we ended up playing happy families like
our parents. If only we'd known, eh?

Anyway, Roy moaned all the way there
about his irreplaceable CDs. I must admit I'd
had enough of 'Wheels on the Bus' by the time
we got there.

Then, when I saw where our tent was, I
was so upset. Right in the shade. Under 200
trees and blitzed with flies. Bleeding hot
sunshine and my kids are sitting in thick fleeces,
long trousers and woolly socks. It was bloody
freezing. I marched up to the camp site owner
and complained. Said we'd get bloody
pneumonia. I pointed at the picture of the camp
site in the brochure. There wasn't a tree on it.
Just blue skies and happy families. Kids running
around in their vest and knickers. Anyway he
moved us the second week. To a spot in the
sunshine. So it wasn't so bad. And Roy
managed to master the Calor-Gas stove so I got
a cup of tea in bed every morning.

Lovely scenery. We only left the camp
site one day. Roy wanted to see some old
World War Two ruins. Bunkers. He could have
told us we'd be driving from one end of France
to the other. The kids weren't interested. Just
fought all afternoon. I was relieved to get back
to be honest.

They had a lovely time, thanks. We
hardly saw them all holiday. They made friends
with other kids on the site, as you do. We didn't
even see them for meals. Between you and I, I

reckon they got sick of Roy's attempts at dinner on the stove. Tinned sausages and beans. Night after night. Resembled something you wouldn't give an animal.

Local wine? Oh, amazing. Like nectar. Never tasted anything like it. The camp site had a shop which sold bottles made at a local vineyard. Slept like a log most nights. Well after Roy had his oats. He was like a rabid dog. Couldn't keep it down.

Must have been all that bare flesh on the camp site which got him going. No sooner had my head hit the blow up pillow, then he was all over me like a rash. No stopping him. One night I didn't even wake up until he'd nearly finished, which was a relief. He woke me up mumbling something like "Oh Rose, Rose." But I was half asleep, he must have said "Oh stove, stove." The Calor-Gas didn't light that night.

Men. What do you do? Just what they're like, isn't it? Yours the same? Would have thought they'd have grown out of it by now.

Anyway, luckily Roy doesn't take too long these days. Thank goodness he's not into foreplay. Just rolls on and rolls off. Suits me. Not one for all this licking of ears and toes.

But my back. I couldn't stand up straight for a week after that camp bed and the car journeys. I said to Roy, I'm not doing that again.

You went to Italy? A villa? And childcare? Oh it must have been wonderful. Time to yourself? I never have a wink.

I start back at work full-time when the kids are back at school. Yes, still at the local council. They've amalgamated two departments to cut costs. Marketing and PR. So I'm boss of both now. Just the two of us in the department. Quite nice really. Easier work than looking after kids. Nobody bothers us much. Nothing goes on in Leicestershire anyhow, thank goodness. So we tootle along.

Anyway, the reason I'm calling. You'll never guess what? *(Pause)* Two weeks ago I got a wracking pain in my groin. I thought Roy must have strained my muscle on holiday when he clambered aboard. He has put on a lot of weight after the children. Looks like a pregnant duck these days. I've put him on a calorie controlled diet. No carbohydrates and a packed lunch for work every day.

So I went to the doctor. Said it feels like the pain you have after eating a good curry. You know all full and bloated and painful to the touch. He put me on some pills but the pain got worse. So I went back and he prodded me about some more.

"You're pregnant," he announced. Great big smile on his face. "For fuck's sake," I said.

Well, I rang Roy straight away. He nearly choked on his packed lunch when I told him. "Fuck's sake," he said. He was that delighted. Luckily a colleague was with him because I heard some woman in the background telling him to take deep breaths and banging him on his back.

101

We're over the moon. Two months gone now. Can't wait. I've already started getting some of the baby clothes out. And packing my hospital bag.

You too? No! Well, isn't that a coincidence. So you're extending the nanny's hours. Course, you'll need to with three.

Oh, we don't mind as long as it's healthy. Boy or a girl. Oh, I can hear Roy. Yes, it is late. He works so hard these days. Even so, every night after dinner he's straight out in the garden working on the arbour. He's such a good man.

You must come round when it's finished. A little get together. Yes, and Andrew.

Lovely to chat, Julia. Congratulations on your news. Speak soon. Bye love, bye.

Kate Delamere

The Widow's Might

She refused my gown ... the ungrateful cow! I said to Neville, you don't need to go to the expense of buying a wedding dress, when mine is still perfectly good ... perfectly pretty ... divine. When I married Neville's father in 1964 the gown was very *haute couture* like nothing produced today ... all tat! And as for the jewellery ... I did so want them to have mine. I pleaded with her, I said it would be an honour and it would maintain the continuity of family ...

the love.   I do think that fine jewellery expresses love and commitment between couples. She still refused. Later I heard from my son, after a very distressing *contretemps*, that Sarah considered me to be a control freak … me a control freak … whatever that sordid little phrase may mean … I was so upset … my generosity cast back at me … that guttersnipe's so unfeeling.   For God's sake, I was offering her my wedding gown … she has no sensitivity to the connotations …. It had to go … take on a new life … it brought back too many painful memories … I had offered her my engagement ring and wedding ring too! … again to no avail … she is so insensitive, so ungracious …. I hate her and her pernicious influence on my son … but I got my revenge.

One day, just a week before the service, whilst Sarah was engaged in some intricate work … sewing or the like … however, she couldn't do it with her engagement ring on … that's how much she values the sanctity of that symbol … she took it off and laid it heartlessly on the arm of the chair. I saw my chance … I was compelled by some gratifying force … she was so engaged that she didn't notice … and I took the ring up and pocketed it quickly. Within seconds I formulated my plot for revenge …. I knew where Neville had stored the wedding ring for safe keeping and I had access to the gown.   I made an excuse to Sarah … saying something about an appointment in town and I left the room … with the engagement ring securely in my pocket … and went upstairs to collect the other ring and that infernal dress … she really doesn't have any taste … white lace at her age! Returning downstairs, I quickly left the house, making sure not to disturb Sarah, and flung the goods in the boot of the car. Filled with an air of implacable triumph, I drove very quickly into town and found the nearest charity shop.

"Hello, dear," said a drab little old lady from among piles of hideous bric-a-brac … the stench of the unwashed and their filthy cast offs made me retch …. "I'd like to leave these with you," I replied and I handed her the rings and the dress. I received the crone's gratitude curtly and left. I felt relieved … now that silly little bitch will have to avail herself of my offer … or not marry my Neville.

David McCormack

The Lilac Tree Garden

What does he do out there all day, that's what I'd like to know? Digging, weeding, cutting, tying things up.

He didn't show so much attention to me all those years ago. Now, girl – that's enough, what's done is done. He'll be in just now with his dirty boots, walking across my kitchen floor. He doesn't realise how much it hurts my knees to get down to clean it.

I'll leave his cup of tea by the door, he'll know I've made some, he'll have heard the kettle whistling.

I knew it! There he goes, straight into the kitchen, never thinks to wipe his feet. Messing up my hard work. What would he say if I chopped the heads off his flowers? It's the same thing really. Come to think – he wouldn't say anything. I mean, why break the habit of twenty-four years?

Is it really that long since we last spoke together? Time flies by so quickly. Perhaps we should have parted. Why didn't we? Like old shoes I suppose. They're just there, you have to make an effort to throw them out.

Why did he shut me out? Didn't he know I wanted to talk about it – to cry? Hard, that's what he is, doesn't care. Maybe it would have been different if it had been a boy. A man's pride always makes him want a son first. I wonder why? If the child had been a boy he would have cared then – maybe. But a girl, well, it didn't matter did it? Me? I just wanted her to live.

When they told me she was dead, I went cold, numb. I wish I'd gone to the funeral. I should have made him take me, but he let doctors tell him what to do. How could they know what was best and he didn't care what I wanted?

I felt her being lowered into the ground. We ought to have been there together. I needed his hand to hold as they covered her over, surely he could see that. When he came back, I turned away. If I couldn't have his understanding, I certainly didn't want his pity.

That's when we stopped speaking. He hasn't taken me to see where she is buried. He goes, I know he does.

And that blasted garden. Oh! It was going to be such a wonderful place for our child, with grass, a swing, a slide and a sandpit. He was going to put lilac trees everywhere. The child would grow up with lilac trees all around him, 'him' you notice. He was going to know how we met when the lilac bloomed.

*

Her birthday is in May. There was a lilac tree in bloom just down the road, I couldn't bear to look at it for years. And that's another thing, he knew how I felt about lilac after the baby died and what did he do? He went and asked for some cuttings, came home whistling. He planted those cuttings all over the garden. I hated him for that. The garden is full of flowers but somehow it's empty; funny, though, those lilac trees have never bloomed. God's judgment, I dare say.

Well, he's got his garden and I've got Lucy. I remember how pleased she was about the baby. She looked forward to having a cousin to play with. It would have been like having a brother or sister she said. But as things turned out …. Never mind, she has a baby girl now and well, it's like having a grandchild.

He doesn't like me knitting for the baby; I can tell by the way he looks at me when I sit in the chair with the wool and pins. He pulled the stitches off the needles the other day, just spite it was. I know it was him, I mean, who else is there?

I haven't been in the garden for a while now. The yard's big enough for the washing and I can't bear to see the garden so empty. I wonder why he bothers with it?

Well! I don't believe it. Here he comes, walking right through the house this time and with his muddy boots. He really is too much! Now what? What's he pointing at? Better go and see. This is what comes of not speaking, my girl.

*

If I speak I shall cry. Why didn't he tell me he'd stopped those trees from blooming all these years? Now the garden is full of lilac and I want to cry. He ought to have told me he'd planted it in memory of our little girl. It seems he'd stopped them blooming until I was ready to bear the memory. He says Lucy's little girl can grow up with the scent of lilac in May.

We're going to choose a swing and a slide together and next week the sand is coming. He's sorry about the knitting, he'd only wanted to look, never seen anything so small.

Why did he choose to let the lilac bloom this year, and why show me today of all days, twenty-five years to the day when we first met?

I wonder if he remembers.

Josie Elson

AFTERWORD AND ACKNOWLEDGEMENTS

Afterword and Acknowledgements

In her Preface, Deborah Tyler-Bennett suggests that one of the pleasures of anthologies like this one is 'diversity.' As she goes on to imply, however, this diversity is also marked by connectiveness – as, for example, in the portrayals of city landscapes in Leigh Chia's 'Sepulchral City' and Sue Mackrell's vision of Prague. The pleasure of diversity is also the pleasure of finding connections, often in places where they aren't expected. In helping to compile this anthology, I have enjoyed tracing connections, images and themes between the works selected. As with the portrayals of the 'city,' a large number of the works have geographical themes (see those by David Bircumshaw, Maha Mahmoud, Vicky Smith, Mellissa Flowerdew-Clarke and others); some are about inter-generational conflicts (see those by David McCormack, Kate Delamere and myself); and very many are about love and sexual relationships (see those by Jodie Clark, Maria D. Orthodoxou, Josie Elson, Robin Webber-Jones, Kate Delamere, and so on and so forth).

No doubt there are reasons for these shared themes. By definition, an anthology devoted to 'Words for Speaking Aloud' is going to elicit certain kinds of writing: love poetry is bound to be prevalent, since a great deal of it is surely written to be read aloud to someone else. Similarly, monologues are bound to be prevalent, particularly in the 'Words for Performing' section. No doubt there are other reasons for shared concerns: many of these pieces started life in the same creative writing workshops from the same exercises. And no doubt, in part, the connections I've drawn between texts are constructed by my own mind. Hopefully, other readers will find many other pleasurable connections of their own between the works – as well as, indeed, disjunctions and disconnections. In reading and experiencing an anthology like this, the reader should allow the pieces to speak to one another, jostle with one another, disagree with one another, link with one another, even mate with one another.

Finally, it remains for Robin Webber-Jones and I to express thanks to all those who helped make the *Speaking Words* project so exciting, in workshops, in live events, and in this anthology. Thanks must go to the tutors of the dayschools – Gareth Watts, Mystie Hood, Maria Orthodoxou, Mitzi Szereto, Deborah Tyler-Bennett, Robin Webber-Jones, Tony Coult – and, just as importantly, to the participants. Thanks to all those who submitted work for the anthology; whether ultimately accepted or not, all the work submitted was of a high standard and was a pleasure to read. Thanks and best wishes to Deborah Tyler-Bennett for her hard work in editing this collection. Many thanks to Linda Young for her art-work. Thanks to the Department of English and Drama, Loughborough University, BBC Radio Leicester and Monks' Dyke Technology College for the use of their resources and space. Thanks to Loughborough University Arts Centre for their help with publicity. And, of course, thanks to the Awards for All scheme of the National Lottery who funded the project.

Jonathan Taylor, 2005

NOTE ON CRYSTAL CLEAR CREATORS

Crystal Clear Creators is a not-for-profit organisation which develops, records and showcases new and established talent for radio, including writers, voice-overs and producers. It has recorded radio drama, poetry and prose. It is developing links with radio stations across the region as well as with the B.B.C. Its members' work has been broadcast on various radio stations, locally and nationally. It has hosted various public events in Loughborough, Leicester and Lincolnshire. Its website is www.crystalclearcreators.org.

Crystal Clear Creators is funded by the Arts Council England, National Lottery, Riverside Midlands, Ernest Cook Foundation and many other bodies. Crystal Clear Creators has now set up a publishing imprint, Crystal Clear Creators (CCC) Publishing.

If you would like to find out more about Crystal Clear Creators' work, or would like to join the organisation, please contact Jonathan Taylor at J.P.Taylor1@lboro.ac.uk. Crystal Clear Creators is always looking for new writers, performers and producers for members; it is also always looking to record and produce new work. As a member, you are entitled to have your work considered for recording and broadcasting via the website.

CONTRIBUTORS' NOTES

Susan Bell is married with three sons and currently lives in Nottinghamshire. She graduated from Loughborough University in 1994 and is currently writing up her PhD thesis which concerns Thomas Hardy and composers who set his words to music.

David Bircumshaw crashed landed here from the birth-drop some 50 years ago in Warwickshire. From time to time, he remembers parts of his life. He has published in magazines in the UK, US and Australia. He has two small collections: *Painting Without Numbers* (2002) and *The Animal Subsides* (2004). He edits the online occasional magazine *A Chide's Alphabet*. He lives on income support in central Leicester among many very, very eccentric people.

Julie Boden, a Birmingham Poet Laureate, Co-Director of 'Poetry Central' and currently 'Poet in Residence at Symphony Hall, Birmingham,' has written five collections of poetry which are popular at home and abroad and this has led her to perform, conduct workshops and judge poetry competitions internationally. Julie has been filmed for a number of poetry programmes for TV and has appeared on National Radio including Radio Four's 'Women's Hour' and 'Front Row' and Radio 3's 'The Verb.' A regular guest on local radio, she works hard to promote the voices of other Midlands' poets.

Jodie Clark is a PhD student at Loughborough University, researching the relationships between language, community and sexuality. She is originally from St. Michaels, Maryland, USA and has also lived in Paris (teaching English) and Strasbourg (running a study abroad programme).

Kate Delamere is a former national newspaper, magazine and television journalist, who now combines writing with teaching in creative writing and journalism. She is currently co-writing a project for Leicester's Haymarket and Phoenix theatres and has just finished her first novel, with a London agent.

Josie Elson is a widow with two grown up sons and one grandaughter. She has been writing for many years but since retiring has given it more time. She mainly writes children's stories but will attempt other genres.

Gabriel Eshun is a Ghanaian, currently a researcher at doctoral level at the Geography Department of the University of Leicester, UK. He has recorded his work with Crystal Clear Creators.

Mellissa Flowerdew-Clarke is an aspiring playwright and a recent graduate of the MA in Modern & Contemporary Writing at Loughborough University. She is the 2005 winner of the Crystal Clear Creators 'Soliloquized' competition, and her poetry is published in Dead Letter Office webzine and Machio magazine. Her playwriting is inspired by 'in-yer-face' theatre and her theatrical work has been performed at Watersmeet Theatre, Rickmansworth.

Mark Goodwin lives in Leicestershire, where he works as a community poet. His poetry & fiction have been published in a wide range of literary magazines & webzines. He received an Eric

Gregory Award from the Society of Authors in 1998. Working with poet Deborah Tyler-Bennett, Mark edited *Poetry, Prose and Playfullness for Teachers & Learners*, published by Leicestershire County Council.

Radcliff Gregory has written three books of poetry under a pseudonym: *Fragile Art, Figaro's Cabin* and *Everywhere, Except....* He has also been anthologised in several poetry magazines and multi-author collections, including *Coffee House*. Radcliff also writes non-fiction articles on literature, disability and identity issues, and has begun researching his first novel.

Robin Hamilton was born in 1947, brought up mostly in Glasgow, taught English for twenty years at Loughborough University before retiring, early, to live the good life. He has two children, one ex-wife, and a bonzai. *The Lost Jockey: Collected Poems 1966-1982* was published in 1985. He is currently proprietor of The Phantom Rooster Press. His exemplar is James Crichton ['The Admirable Crichton'] (1560-1582), Scottish poet, intellectual paragon, and swordsman. Robin Hamilton's *Pacts and Conjurations: New and Selected Poems* is due to be published from Arrowhead Press later this year (2005).

Mystie Hood is an American writer who is currently doing a Ph.D in Creative Writing. She is writing her first novel, after writing short stories for many years, including on an M.A. writing programme in the U.S.

Sue Mackrell is an MA student on the Creative Writing programme at Loughborough University. She has had poems published in a range of anthologies and magazines. She has taught Creative Writing and English to students with special needs, and run workshops with community groups. She is currently teaching in a Further Education College in Coventry.

Maha Mahmoud is a writer and poet from Sudan, who has just completed her M.A. in Creative Writing at Loughborough University.

David McCormack was born in London in 1954. He holds an honours degree in English and Drama and a Master's from the Shakespeare Institute. Formerly an actor and director, he now teaches at a National College for the disabled in Coventry. He is a prolific writer of poetry and he has recently begun work on a tetralogy of plays on historic political figures for radio.

Maria D. Orthodoxou is a teacher of English in Leicester. She has had her poetry published in various magazines, and has performed her work in venues across the Midlands. She was one of the tutors on the creative writing dayschools for *Speaking Words*. Amongst other on-going projects, she has recently been involved in scriptwriting for a musical to be put on at the Leicester Haymarket. She also acts, and has appeared in various productions for Crystal Clear Creators.

Victoria Rose Poolman comes from a small village in north Hampshire and is currently studying for her creative writing MA at Loughborough University. With a keen interest in journalism, travel writing, song writing and poetry, she hopes to pursue a career in one of these areas when she graduates in 2006. When she's not putting pen to paper, Victoria loves music, the theatre, skiing and travelling – which she hopes to do much more of in the future ... purely for inspiration of course!

Mark Pullinger spent his childhood avoiding reading at all costs. Then, upon leaving school, he discovered the world that is literature. The discovery ignited a passion to interact with that world, to live in it. In his twenties, he found himself in his first anthology and, with that sense of belonging, he has breathed in that world ever since.

Louise Pymer writes poetry, prose and plays and has no particular favourite – she likes to be as free with the genre as possible and use the idea to determine which to use. She has always been passionate about writing and reading, wanting to escape to someone else's world, or help others to escape to her own characters'.

She has produced a great deal of work over her Creative Writing Master's in the last year at Loughborough University, and hopes to get her dissertation, 'Emotional Thump,' published.

Kate Sharp enjoyed her BA English at Loughborough so much that she stayed for the Creative Writing MA, which she's just completed. She now lives in Cheltenham, composing poems about Bradgate Park (Leicestershire), and baking cake!

Vicky Smith is a keen traveller and photographer whose wanderlust inspires much of her poetry and prose. Following a degree in Drama with English and a Master's in Modern and Contemporary Literature, specialising in Creative Writing, Vicky now works in publishing. As a member of Crystal Clear Creators, she has recorded and performed her poems and given writing workshops.

Jonathan Taylor is co-founder and co-director of Crystal Clear Creators. He is also a lecturer in English at Loughborough University, where he is convenor of the M.A. in Creative Writing. He has had stories published in various magazines. His radio plays have been produced by Crystal Clear Creators and broadcast on various stations. He is currently completing a novel-length memoir about his father.

Deborah Tyler-Bennett is author of the collection *Clark Gable in Mansfield* (Rotherham: King's England, 2003). A wide selection of her work appears in *Take Five* (Nottingham: Shoestring, 2003), and she co-edited (with Mark Goodwin), *Poetry, Prose, and Playfulness for Teachers and Learners* (Leics County Council Press, 2004). She edits the journal, *The Coffee House*, and takes part in many writing projects including the Organworks at Eton College Project for state schools. With Gillian Spraggs she is co-author of a web package for the Victoria and Albert Museum. Having had over 300 poems and short fictions published in international journals and anthologies, she is currently working on a second collection.

Nathan Vaughan is currently completing his PhD at Loughborough University. His many influences include: James Herbert, Dean Koontz and, of course, Stephen King. His undergraduate dissertation on King was a recipient of the 'Carlton Broadcasting Prize' for best dissertation. An ardent reader of fiction, he would one day like to be a novelist.

Gareth Watts is a 23-year-old Creative Writing PhD student, studying at Loughborough University. Although his Research Project involves writing fictional prose, he remains passionate about poetry, and loves to write performance poetry as well as lyric poems for his pop band 'Tokyo Beatbox.' Gareth is also currently writing a comedy pilot for Rutland Radio.

Robin Webber-Jones is a producer and course writer and developer for the creative industries. He is also co-founder of Crystal Clear Creators. Originally born in Lincolnshire he soon gathered a love of poetry and is delighted to be included in this collection of works.

Xanthe Wells is in the final year of a fictocritical PhD that examines the work of Virginia Woolf and Jeanette Winterson. She enjoys working with new genres and believes in the beauty of language, both in poetry and prose. Xanthe has also written for local magazines and takes a keen interest in script-writing.